HAL LEONARD
GUITAR METHOD
Supplement to Any Guitar Method

ROCK GUITAR
Learn to Play Rhythm and Lead Rock Guitar with
Step-by-Step Lessons and 70 Great Rock Songs

By Michael Mueller

Recording Credits:
Doug Boduch, Guitar
Scott Schroedl, Drums
Eric Hervey, Bass
Warren Wiegratz, Keyboards

ISBN 0-634-04772-8

7777 W. BLUEMOUND RD. P.O. BOX 13819 MILWAUKEE, WI 53213

Visit Hal Leonard Online at
www.halleonard.com

CONTENTS

INTRODUCTION

Welcome to the Hal Leonard Rock Guitar method. This book is designed not only as a supplement to the Hal Leonard Guitar Method, but can also stand on its own in teaching the basic techniques necessary to get you started playing rock guitar. As you begin working through this book, you'll immediately notice what it is that sets this rock guitar method apart. To demonstrate each concept in the book, we use real rock songs— no corny rock arrangements of "Londonderry Air" here! You want to learn to play in the style of your favorite rock artists, including Eric Clapton, the Beatles, the Rolling Stones, and more, so what better way to learn than by playing excerpts of your favorite rock songs to demonstrate the lesson at hand. Now, let's get started.

TABLATURE

Guitar players have long used a number system called *tablature*, or "tab" for short, as a means of guitar notation. Tablature consists of six horizontal lines, each representing a string on the guitar. The top line represents the high E string, second line the B string, third line the G string, and so on. A number on the line indicates the fret number at which you play the note.

Though tablature has had an immeasurable effect on learning guitar and songs, it does have one major weakness: it doesn't indicate the rhythm of the notes. You'll have to refer to the standard notation to obtain the correct rhythm for each example. Though there are new versions of tab that put stems on the numbers to indicate rhythm, these are no substitute for learning to read music. So, bite the bullet and learn what those little black dots mean (see the *Hal Leonard Guitar Method, Book 1*). It'll pay off in the long run.

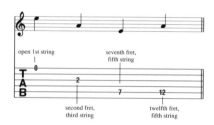

ABOUT THE AUDIO

At the end of each chapter in the Hal Leonard Rock Guitar method, there is a song with which you can jam along. The enclosed audio CD contains a full-band accompaniment for each of these songs. The corresponding track number for each song is listed below the audio icon 🔊 .

The purpose of these Jam Sessions is for you to practice both the rhythm and lead studies you learn in each chapter. As such, jam along with the rhythm track for each song, and when you feel ready, play solos where indicated using the licks and techniques from the Lead Study section.

ACOUSTIC VS. ELECTRIC

Though most of the songs in this book contain electric guitar parts, don't let it hinder you from digging in if all you currently have is an acoustic guitar. Acoustic and electric guitars, in terms of learning chords, scales, and the fingerings, are the same instrument. Some of the techniques, such as bending strings, lend themselves better to performance on an electric guitar, but you can still learn just as effectively on your acoustic guitar.

CHOOSING AN ELECTRIC GUITAR AND AMP

If you're in the market for your first electric guitar and amplifier, there are a few things you should consider before dropping a month's salary on the same gear as your favorite guitar hero. First of all, you don't have to break the bank to get quality gear. An electric guitar will set you back anywhere from $70 to $7,000—or more for a vintage jewel. The same is true for amps. Before you take out a second mortgage on your home or ask your parents for your college trust fund money, realize that it's not too difficult to find a guitar and amp combo that will suit your needs for as little as $300. Go to several dealers in your area and do some comparison shopping.

Next, you need to decide what style of guitar and amp you want to buy. Given that this is a rock guitar book, there are four general guitar styles you may wish to consider. These are Strat-style, Tele-style, Les Paul-style, and hollowbody or semi-hollowbody guitars. The style of guitar you choose will have a lot to do with the specific rock subgenre you favor. For example, if you are a classic rock fanatic, a Les Paul-style guitar may be for you. Each, however, has its own distinct sound and feel, so be sure to check them all out and choose the one that is right for you.

In choosing your amp, you basically have two choices: tube or solid-state. Tube amps are so-named because they are powered by and get their tonal characteristics from vacuum tubes, whereas solid-state amps use transistors for power and tone. What does this mean to you? Well, conventional wisdom says that tube amps provide a more three-dimensional sound than their solid-state counterparts and are thus favored amps among the pros, but they are also more prone to subtle idiosyncrasies that may befuddle a beginning guitarist looking for simplicity. The reality is that on a beginner's budget, you're likely to get more bang for your buck with a solid-state amp. But, as with the guitars, try both, and choose the one that best suits your needs. Regardless of which you choose, however, you will want an amp with two channels—clean and distorted—to satisfy the needs of being a rock guitar player. Be sure to get a footswitch, too!

Gibson Les Paul guitar with Marshall amp.

Fender Stratocaster guitar with
Fender Twin Reverb amp.

CHAPTER 1: OPEN CHORDS

RHYTHM STUDY

Open-position chords are quite often the first step in a budding guitarist's musical journey. Often referred to as "cowboy chords" due to their prominence in early country and western music, they should not be dismissed as merely elementary. Played near the nut and possessing a big, hardy sound, open chords serve as the foundation for many of rock's biggest hits.

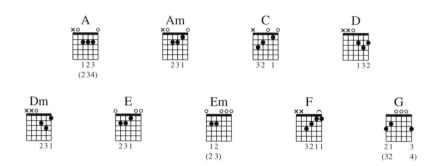

These chords are most typically played with a *strumming* technique. Using either downstrokes or upstrokes (or both), every note in the chord is played with one smooth pick stroke. The next example uses an eighth-note strum pattern, which requires you to play alternating downstrokes and upstrokes. Remember to play all the notes of the chord with each strum.

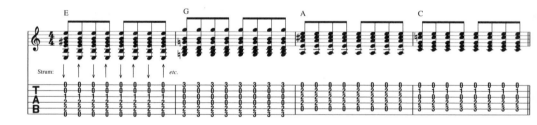

In the previous example, did you find yourself hesitating each time you had to move to a new chord? If so, don't feel bad; it's a challenge that all beginning guitarists encounter and eventually overcome. The ability to seamlessly change chords in time is one of the most important skills you'll develop as a guitarist. And since open chords are among the most prominent in rock music, now is a good time to start.

Here are a couple of key elements in changing open chords. First, look for common tones and fingerings between chords. For example, check out the fingerings for the C major and A minor chords.

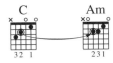

Both chords are played on the top five strings; both chords contain an open high E string; both chords are fretted on the second string at the first fret with your index finger; finally, both chords are fretted on the fourth string at the second fret with your middle finger. So, if you're going to change from C to Am, all you need do is lift your ring finger off the fifth string at the third fret and place it on third string at the second fret, and then play the open fifth string as part of the Am chord. Vóila! It's that simple. To go from Am to C, reverse the action.

The second technique that comes in extremely handy when changing chords is strumming open strings for one portion of the beat before the change. To demonstrate, let's practice changing from D to G while strumming in an eighth-note rhythm. If you examine the two chords in the progression below, you'll see that there are no common fingerings, so switching between these two chords may represent a slightly greater challenge than the Am–C progression. However, if you lift your fingers off the D shape on the last eighth note of the measure and simply strum a few of the open strings, you'll buy yourself a little time to get them back down onto the fretboard for the G chord on the downbeat.

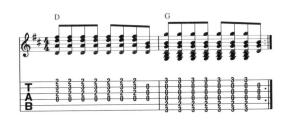

Okay, you're only in Chapter 1 and—though you may not realize it—you already have the tools necessary to create a hit song! If you don't believe me, take a look at the following songs. Practice them slowly using a metronome, and gradually increase the tempo until you can play them up to speed without mistakes or hesitation on the chord changes.

RUN AROUND

Words and Music by John Popper
Copyright © 1994 BLUES TRAVELER PUBLISHING CORP.
All Rights Administered by IRVING MUSIC, INC.

TWIST AND SHOUT

MAGGIE MAY

TIME FOR ME TO FLY

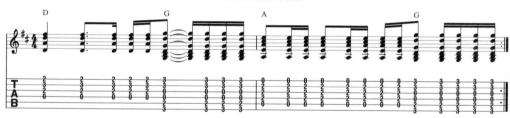

EAD STUDY

fixture of the guitar-based rock 'n' roll song is the guitar solo. Guitar solos are created by playing notes from scale, which is an organized set of notes that belong to a key. By far, the most prominent scale in rock 'n' roll music is the *minor pentatonic* scale. This five-note scale has one particular fingering shape that has been used more licks, riffs, and solos than one could possibly imagine.

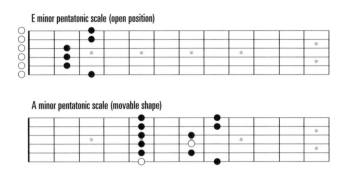

E minor pentatonic scale (open position)

A minor pentatonic scale (movable shape)

o play the movable form of this scale, fret all the notes at the fifth fret with your index finger, the notes on e seventh fret (strings 3, 4, and 5) with your ring finger, and the notes at the eighth fret (strings 1, 2, and 6) ith your pinky finger. This fingering is especially good for beginning guitarists because it builds strength and exterity in the typically weak, uncoordinated pinky finger.

ou could also "cheat" by using your stronger, more dextrous ring finger in place of your pinky finger for the otes on the eighth fret. This is a common technique among rock and blues guitarists, but if you choose to arn in this manner, the only thing you'll be cheating is your overall skill. That said, I highly recommend using our pinky finger to play those notes as you work through the following licks:

E minor pentatonic licks

A minor pentatonic licks

BENDING

By far one of the most common and requisite techniques of rock guitar, bending a string raises the pitch of the fretted note without having to change positions on the guitar. Half- and whole-step bends are the most common types, though you can bend to any interval you want—as long as your fingers are strong enough!

Besides building strength in your fingers, the other real challenge of bending strings is hitting the right pitch, or intonation. At first, your bends may sound out of tune, but with practice, you'll be able to hit them just right. Here's a tip for developing proper intonation on your bends. Let's say, for example, that you want to bend the D note on the third string at the seventh fret up one whole step to the pitch of E. First, fret the D note with your ring finger and sound the note. Then, slide up to the E note at the ninth fret and listen closely to the difference in pitch between the two notes. Do this a few times. Got it? Good. Now, play the D note again, but this time, bend the string until the pitch matches the fretted E note. *Tip: Use your index and middle fingers to help you bend the string up to pitch. Try the following must-know minor pentatonic rock licks.

Here are two classic rock guitar riffs that contain bends and are also based on the minor pentatonic scale.

SUSIE-Q

Words and Music by Dale Hawkins, Stan Lewis and Eleanor Broadwater
Copyright © 1957 (Renewed) by Arc Music Corporation (BMI)

RUMBLE

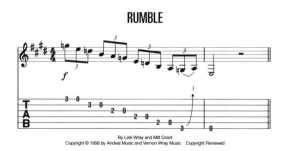

By Link Wray and Milt Grant
Copyright © 1958 by Andval Music and Vernon Wray Music   Copyright Renewed

...ally, one of the benefits of bending strings is that it helps you to be more expressive in your lines. And true
...form, the signature sounds of many of rock 'n' roll's most expressive songs stem from string bending.

SOMETHING

SLEEPWALK

WONDERFUL TONIGHT

JAM SESSION

Congratulations! You've nearly reached the end of Chapter 1. Time to recap: You've learned the most import open chords, the most commonly used scale, and a handful of cool licks. Now, it's time to jam. And what be way to start jamming than with a song by perhaps the greatest "jammer" ever: Carlos Santana. The spiritual stormed back onto the scene in 1999 and scored the biggest hit of his career with "Smooth," but it was early, Latin-flavored rock sounds of "Oye Como Va" and "Evil Ways" that lifted him to his heralded position the pantheon of guitar gods.

Try jamming along with the rhythm track for "Oye Como Va" until you can play the chord changes with mistakes. Then, when you're ready, kick your guitar into "Carlos" mode and go crazy using the licks y learned earlier in this chapter as well as your own A minor pentatonic creations.

OYE COMO VA

TRACK 2

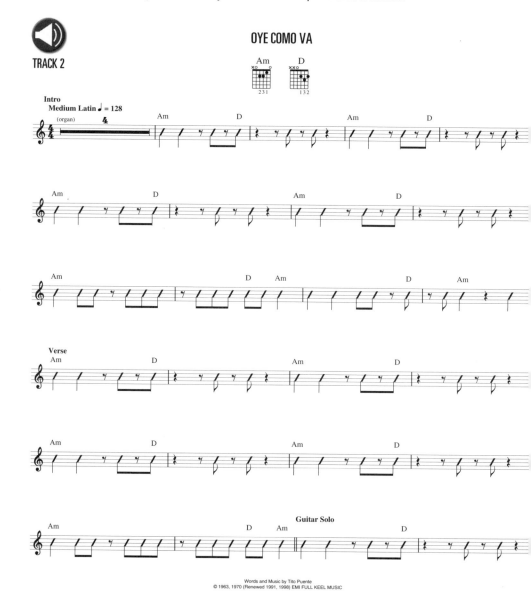

Words and Music by Tito Puente
© 1963, 1970 (Renewed 1991, 1998) EMI FULL KEEL MUSIC

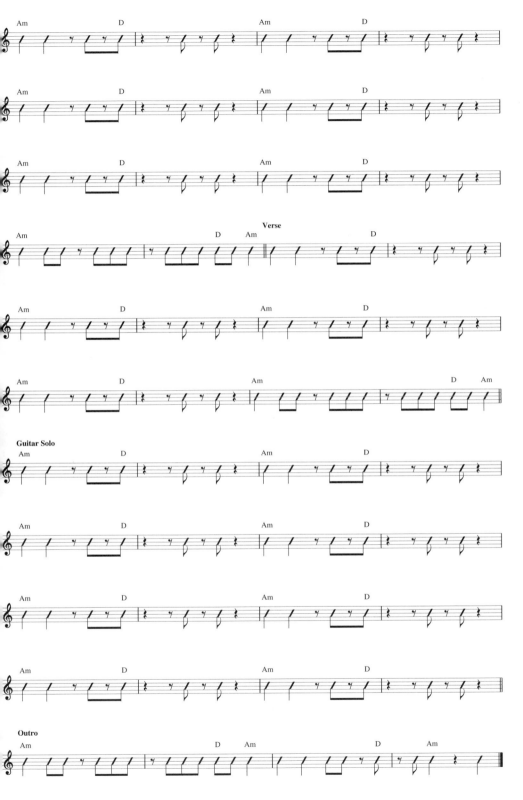

CHAPTER 2: POWER CHORDS

RHYTHM STUDY

Along with open chords, the most prominent chord type found in rock music is the *power chord*. As its nam
implies, the power chord has a very strong, matter-of-fact sound. It is comprised of only two notes: the r
and the fifth of the major scale, and as such, has no definitive major or minor tonality. One of the many c
things about power chords is that they can be played anywhere on the neck. And perhaps the most welcon
thing about power chords at this stage of your learning process is that they're incredibly easy to play. Below a
the fingerings for the three power chords found in open position and the most common movable shape.

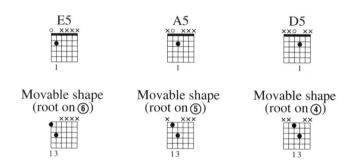

If there is one song in the annals of rock music that best represents the power chord, hands-down it's "Ir
Man" by Black Sabbath. To play "Iron Man" as it sounds on the record, you'll need to take your newfou
power-chord skills and combine them with the "slide" technique that's presented in the lead guitar section
this chapter. If you'd like, you can play it without the slides for now.

IRON MAN

Words and Music by Frank Iommi, John Osbourne, William Ward and Terence Butler
© Copyright 1970 (Renewed) and 1974 (Renewed) Westminster Music Ltd., London, England
TRO - Essex Music International, Inc., New York, controls all publication rights for the U.S.A. and Canada

Black Sabbath isn't exactly your cup of tea, the power chord is prevalent in countless mainstream rock songs s well. Below are a few more power-chord goodies you might recognize:

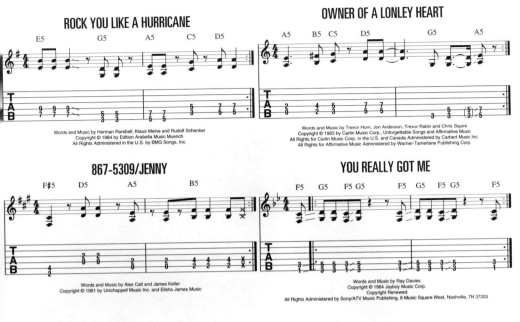

A popular guitar technique that goes hand-in-hand with power chords is *palm muting*. To perform this technique, lightly rest the palm of your picking hand just in front of your guitar's bridge. This will slightly dampen the strings, resulting in a muffled, percussive sound when you pick the strings. When used in conjunction with power chords, it is also common to chug away on the palm-muted bass note, striking the entire power chord on select beats to add rhythmic variety. Check out the excerpts below for some great examples of these techniques.

LEAD STUDY

In chapter 1, we discussed how bending strings can help you be more expressive on the guitar. A second technique with which to make your lines your own is the vibrato technique. *Vibrato* is the rapid alternation of raising and returning to original pitch a ringing note. Quite simply, after you strike a note, all you need to do is "shake" the string back and forth with your frethand finger(s). Be careful not to overdo it and risk the note going out of tune. A tight, somewhat rapid vibrato is what you first want to achieve. Also, you should become proficient at the vibrato technique using any of your frethand fingers. In the figure below, try applying vibrato to the C note using all four fingers.

Here are two minor pentatonic licks with vibrato for your lead guitar repertoire. Try using these when you jam along with "Wild Thing" at the end of this chapter.

The next challenge is to combine your two newfound techniques, bending and vibrato to create something even more special. In the following examples, you'll be bending a note, and while maintaining the bend, you'll apply vibrato, being extra-careful not to push the note sharp or let it fall flat. Remember the tip about using the other fingers on your fret hand to help bend the string? That's especially helpful when applying vibrato to a bent note, so be sure to take advantage of the extra help. Try it with these blues-rock licks.

SLIDES

A favorite technique for moving between two notes on the fretboard is the *slide*. You saw this technique employed in several of the song excerpts in the previous section. There are several variations you can employ when sliding from note to note: You can slide into a note [A]; out of a note [B]; from note to note, picking each one [C]; or from note to note, picking only the first one [D].

In examples A and B above, there is no predetermined start or end point to the slides. These are sometimes called "slides from/to nowhere." Typically, however, you start or finish the slide two to four frets beyond the target note, and they're perfromed quite quickly. Let's try incorporating these slides into a couple of minor pentatonic licks.

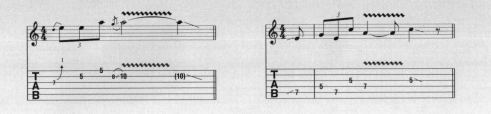

And now, here are a couple of blues-rock classics that utilize slides in their signature intros.

BOOM BOOM

By John Lee Hooker
Copyright © 1962, 1965 (Renewed) by Conrad Music, a division of Arc Music Corp. (BMI)

HEY JOE

Words and Music by Billy Roberts
© 1962 (Renewed) by THIRD PALM MUSIC

JAM SESSION

Hey, you're rockin' now! It's once again time to jam, and to close this chapter, we'll use one of the greatest "jam" songs of all time: "Wild Thing." First recorded by the Troggs, it's probably the one song that *every* guitar player has played at one time or another. It uses four movable power chords, so practice playing those shapes until you can play along with the recording without making mistakes. You can solo over the A5–D5–E5–D5 chord changes using the A minor pentatonic scale when you're ready. Go wild!

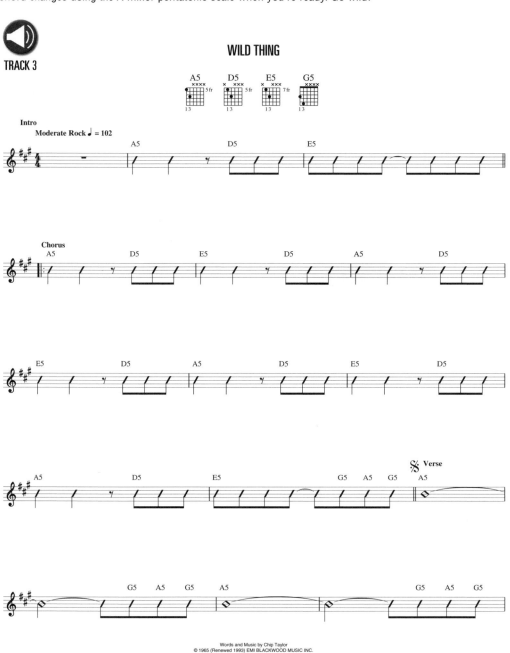

WILD THING

Words and Music by Chip Taylor
© 1965 (Renewed 1993) EMI BLACKWOOD MUSIC INC.

CHAPTER 3: OPEN-POSITION RIFFS

RHYTHM STUDY

Surely, if you're a fan of rock music, you've noticed that the main theme in some of your favorite songs isn't based simply on a chord progression, but rather, on a short, catchy, repeated melodic pattern. This is known as a *riff.* Often, riffs are composed of single-note lines in open position, such as the examples here:

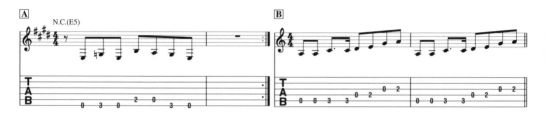

Riffs can also be constructed from open chords or a mixture of open chords and single notes.

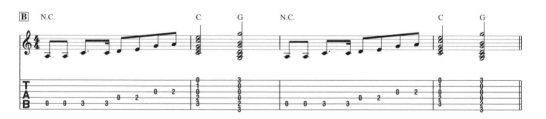

Here are two of the most famous open-position riffs in rock music.

DAY TRIPPER

OH, PRETTY WOMAN

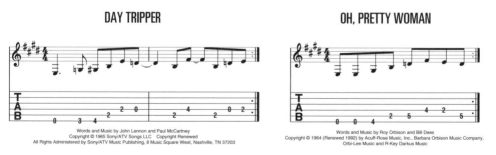

Though riffs are generally comprised of a single-note theme, it is possible to create a chord-based riff. To hear the difference between a basic rhythm guitar part and a chord-based riff, play the next two examples. The first is a simple chord progression. The second is spiced up using embellishments, snappier rhythm, and muted scratches to create a dynamic theme.

Here are a couple of open-chord-based classics:

BLUE ON BLACK

SEMI-CHARMED LIFE

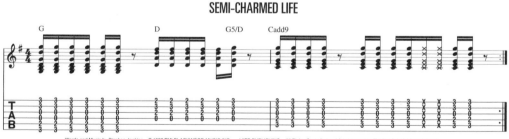

LEAD STUDY

A common goal among beginning guitar players is to be able to play faster—especially solos. One simple way to help you accommodate this desire is a technique called *alternate picking*. Most players, when they first pick up a guitar, will use all downstrokes to play notes and chords, and this will slow you down. If you examine the motion closely, you'll see that to produce the next downstroke, you need to bring the pick back past the string on an upstroke. So why not use that upstroke to strike a note? In effect, picking in a "down-up-down-up" pattern is twice as fast as using all downstrokes.

Below is a quasi-chromatic alternate picking exercise. Start slowly, using a metronome, and gradually increase the tempo as you become comfortable with the alternate picking motion. Continue progressing up the fretboard with this exercise until you reach the twelfth fret. Then, work your way back down.

Let's play through the A minor pentatonic scale you learned earlier, using alternate picking:

The minor pentatonic scale conveniently lays on the fretboard in such a way that you are using a downstroke as you move to each new string. In the "real world," however, this is not always the case. Try using alternate picking in the following examples, which will require you to occasionally play an upstroke when physically moving down to the next string, or a downstroke when physically moving up to the next string. As always, it's best to practice with a metronome to help ensure consistent, precise rhythm.

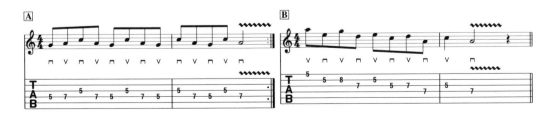

Now, let's revisit a few of the riffs you learned earlier, this time using alternate picking.

DAY TRIPPER

OH, PRETTY WOMAN

Good job! Wasn't that much easier? From now on, use alternate picking in all your licks, riffs, and solos, unless otherwise indicated.

JAM SESSION

For this jam session, let's jam on perhaps the greatest riff ever written: "Day Tripper." You've already learned the main riff of the song, but you'll also need to be able to play it beginning on A and B in order to play along with the track. Practice the three riffs below before beginning.

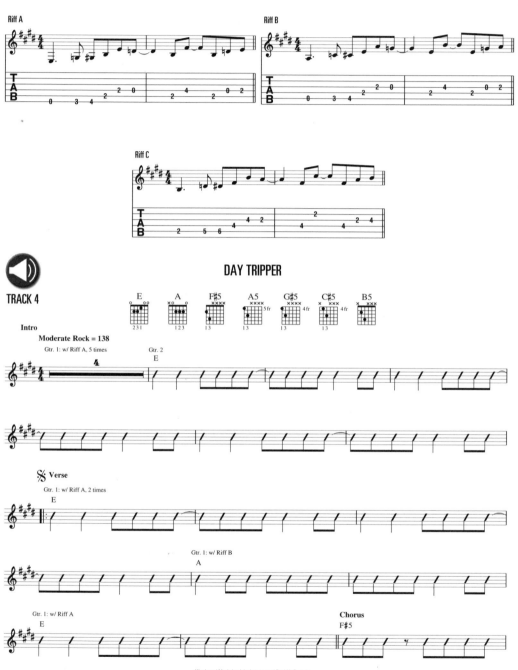

DAY TRIPPER

Words and Music by John Lennon and Paul McCartney
Copyright © 1965 Sony/ATV Songs LLC   Copyright Renewed
All Rights Administered by Sony/ATV Music Publishing, 8 Music Square West, Nashville, TN 37203

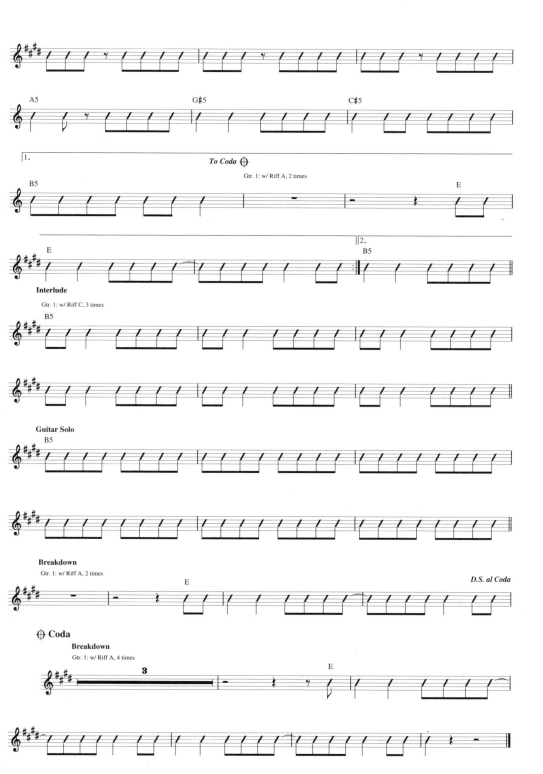

CHAPTER 4: BARRE CHORDS (PART 1)

RHYTHM STUDY

Earlier, we discussed an integral part of rock guitar—the power chord. If you'll remember, there was a movable shape that had its root note in the bass. In this chapter, we're going to explore the barre chords from which the power chords are derived. *Barre chords* get their name from the technique of using your index finger to form a "bar" across the strings. This can be a difficult technique to get down, but when you get it, you'll find it's one of the most rewarding tasks of learning guitar.

The type of barre chord we're going to cover in this chapter is the "E-shape" barre chord. To play this type of chord, first place your fingers in position to play an open E major chord, but use your middle, ring, and pinky fingers to fret the chord. Then, slide up one fret so that the first fret is open. Now, lay your index finger over all six strings at the first fret and press down. When you strum the strings, you should hear an F major chord. To play F minor, simply lift your middle finger off of the G string so that it is played by your index-finger barre. Try playing both chords one-string-at-a-time to be sure that each note rings out. Again, this will take some practice, so please don't let yourself become quickly discouraged.

Movable major shape   Movable minor shape

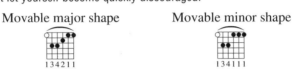

As was previously alluded to, the E-shape barre chord—major and minor—gets its root name from the note on the low E string. Use the diagram below to memorize all the notes on the low E string. This will allow you to quickly find the chords as you read through a piece of music.

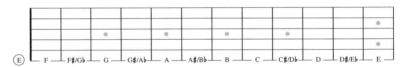

As you've probably noticed, the frets are wider near the nut and gradually become narrower as you move toward the bridge. Practice playing major and minor barre chords all over the fretboard to help you become accustomed to these various fret widths.

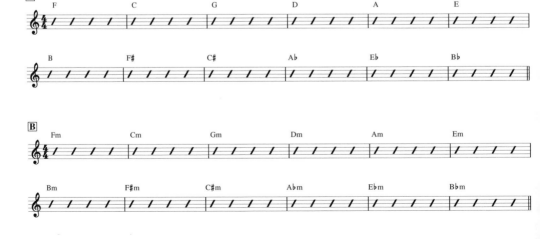

Now, let's try your hand at a few songs using the E-shape barre chord.

FLY AWAY

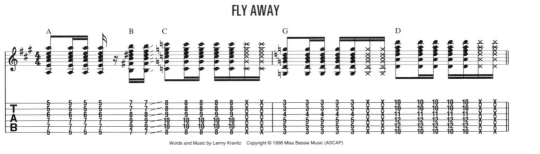

HEAT OF THE MOMENT

TORN

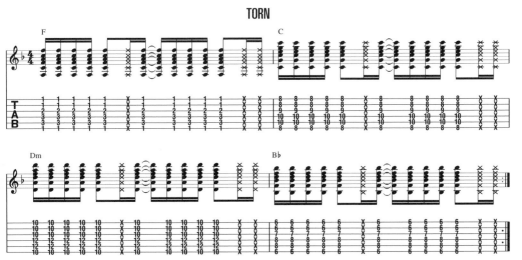

LEAD STUDY

Though the minor pentatonic scale is by far the most prevalent in rock music, major and minor scales also see their fair share of the rock 'n' roll action. Below, you'll find two of the most popular fingerings for each scale as it is used in rock guitar. Remember to use alternate picking as you play through these scales.

Major scale
box pattern

Minor scale
box pattern

Major scale
3-note-per-string pattern

Minor scale
3-note-per-string pattern

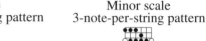

Like the minor pentatonic scale, you can build riffs and solos from the major and minor scales above. Here's a tip to help you avoid a common beginner pitfall: When you play your solo, you don't have to use every note from the scale. Here are a few examples of major and minor scale phrases in some of the most famous rock songs ever. "And I Love Her" contains notes from the F major scale, and "Sweet Child O' Mine" contains notes from the D major scale.

AND I LOVE HER

SWEET CHILD O' MINE

LEGATO

The word *legato* means "smooth." It is a musical term that on guitar translates to two new techniques: *hammer-ons* and *pull-offs*. These two techniques are staples of not only rock guitar but blues, country, jazz, and funk as well. Let's say, for example, that you want to play the notes C and D in succession. You could pick each note, or you can pick the C note, which is fretted with your index finger, and then hammer on to the D note with your ring finger. This produces a smooth transition from one note to the next and gives your picking hand a bit of a break.

Here are a couple of songs that utilize hammer-ons in their signature intros.

PARANOID

HIDE AWAY

Now, let's revisit the C-to-D hammer-on you played earlier, but this time, we're going to move from D to C (see example A). Again, you can either pick each note, or you can first pick the D note, fretted with your ring finger, and then pull that finger off the string (pull-off), thus allowing the C note, which was previously fretted with your index finger, to ring out.

Finally, you can combine these two moves, thus creating a smooth, three-note phrase with only one pick attack (see example B).

Try playing the following famous riffs from Eric Clapton and the Rolling Stones to practice your legato skills.

LAYLA

MISS YOU

JAM SESSION

The rock instrumental established its presence in the late 1950s and early 1960s with the rise in popularity of a new sound: surf rock. One of the biggest hits of the era, "Walk Don't Run," was actually based on a jazz tune written by guitarist Johnny Smith, who simplified the arrangement to fit into the rock combo format of two guitars, bass and drums. The rhythm guitar part uses E-shape barre chords and open chords under the main theme. When you're ready to solo, use the A minor scale and try to squeeze in a generous dose of legato technique.

WALK DON'T RUN

CHAPTER 5: MORE RIFFS

RHYTHM STUDY

Earlier, we discussed open-position riffs. Now, it's time to begin exploring the neck a bit more. Using the scales you've already learned, you can construct any kind of rock guitar riff, limited only by your creative energy. Here are a few famous riffs to get you started in various areas of the neck.

MONEY

Words and Music by Roger Waters
TRO - © Copyright 1973 (Renewed) Hampshire House Publishing Corp., New York, NY

CRAZY TRAIN

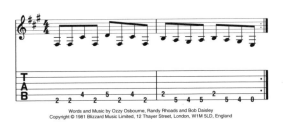

Words and Music by Ozzy Osbourne, Randy Rhoads and Bob Daisley
Copyright © 1981 Blizzard Music Limited, 12 Thayer Street, London, W1M 5LD, England

CARRY ON WAYWARD SON

Words and Music by Kerry Livgren © 1976 EMI BLACKWOOD MUSIC INC. and DON KIRSHNER MUSIC   All Rights Controlled and Administered by EMI BLACKWOOD MUSIC INC.

you learned in Chapter 3, you can use chords to help create riffs, but the chords don't have to be open-position or barre chord configurations. The simplest type of chord is called the *dyad*, which is a two-note chord. In fact, you started playing dyads back in Chapter 2 when you learned how to play a two-note chord called the power chord. Here are two basic power-chord riffs.

further demonstrate both the economy and effectiveness of the dyad, here's one of the most famous and arguably greatest riffs ever penned: "Smoke on the Water."

SMOKE ON THE WATER

Of course, dyads can be combined with single notes to make a great riff, too.

This next example is another of the greatest rock guitar riffs of all time.

SUNSHINE OF YOUR LOVE

Words and Music by Jack Bruce, Pete Brown and Eric Clapton
Copyright © 1968, 1973 by Dratleaf Ltd.   Copyright Renewed
All Rights Administered by Unichappell Music Inc.

LEAD STUDY

The major pentatonic scale can be substituted for the major scale you learned in the previous chapter. It is quite popular in country-rock and Southern-rock styles due to its largely upbeat demeanor. Like its minor cousin, the major pentatonic is also a five-note scale. In fact, if you begin the minor pentatonic scale on its second scale degree and play through to the octave, you'll have just played its relative major pentatonic scale.

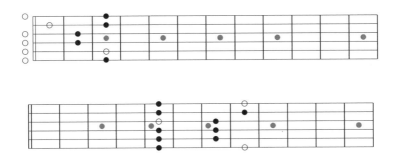

Below are two additional fingerings for the major pentatonic scale. The first is a standard box fingering, and the second covers a larger area of the fretboard. It's easiest to navigate the second fingering utilizing slides between certain notes. These are marked for you in the scale diagram.

Major pentatonic scale box

Major pentatonic scale extended

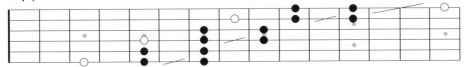

The major pentatonic scale has seen its fair share of the spotlight over the years. You can hear an ascending version in the main riff of the Tempations' "My Girl" and a descending version in the opening guitar lick of the Allman Brothers' "Ramblin' Man."

MY GIRL

RAMBLIN' MAN

This next example is a popular major pentatonic lick in the key of C. It combines the open-position scale pattern with the major pentatonic scale box pattern.

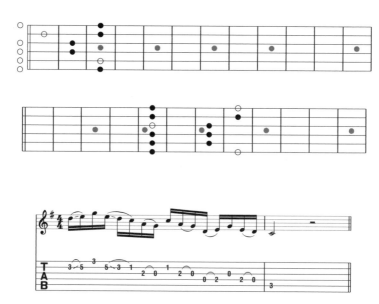

TRILLS

In the last chapter, you learned how to perform hammer-ons and pull-offs. If you rapidly alternate hammer-ons and pull-offs between two notes, you're performing a *trill*. The trill has its roots as an ornamentation in classical music, but over the years has found a special place in the hearts and hands of blues and rock guitarists. Try the following exercise to help develop your trill skill. Be sure to practice this exercise on all six strings and in different positions on the neck.

The most common musical intervals used for trills are minor and major 2nds (half step and whole step, respectively), though trills with minor or major 3rds are equally acceptable. Here is a classic example of the trill used in a blues-rock context, taken from the opening two measures of Stevie Ray Vaughan's "Say What."

SAY WHAT

Written by Stevie Ray Vaughan
© 1985 RAY VAUGHAN MUSIC (ASCAP)/Administered by BUG MUSIC

JAM SESSION

In this chapter's jam session, we've selected a song that eloquently demonstrates how simplicity can take you to great heights. The Beatles' classic, "Drive My Car," is constructed from a simple, single-note riff constructed from the matching major pentatonic scales of the I and IV chords. Practice playing along with the riffs and when you're ready, try using the D major pentatonic scale over the verses, and the B minor pentatonic scale over the chorus. You might recognize that the notes in these two scales are identical; they just start on different scale degrees.

DRIVE MY CAR

CHAPTER 6: BARRE CHORDS (PART 2)

RHYTHM STUDY

Ready for round 2 of barre chords? Good. In this chapter, we're going to learn the basic barre chord forms which the root note is located on the fifth string. These are called the A-shape barre chords, as they allow yo to play the open A chord shape anywhere on the fretboard.

The A-shape chords get their names from the root note on the fifth string. Use the diagram below to memori all the notes on the A string.

You may find the A-shape barre chord a little tougher to play than the E-shape, as this one requires you to barr the second, third, and fourth strings with your ring finger—especially challenging if you want the first strin (barred with your index finger) to ring out too. Here are the chord shapes for both the major and minor forms

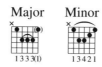

Rather than starting at the first fret, try playing the major chord form at the fifth fret (D major). First, barr your index finger across strings 1–5 at the fifth fret, and allow the tip of your index finger to gently touch th sixth string in order to mute it. Now, lay your ring finger across strings 2–4 at the seventh fret, gently bendin your finger backward a bit at the first knuckle so that the note on the first string at the fifth fret is allowed t ring. If you're having trouble with this last move, it's okay to play only the middle four strings, muting bot the sixth and first strings; however, it will greatly benefit you to be able to sound the note on the first strin as well.

For the minor chord shape, you'll again barre your index finger across strings 1–5 at the fifth fret. Then, plac your ring finger on string 4 at the seventh fret; your pinky finger goes on string 3 at the seventh fret; and you middle finger should be placed on string 2 at the sixth fret. Again, the high A note on string 1 at the fifth fre should be allowed to ring. Strum the top five strings, and you've just played a D minor chord.

You can practice playing the major and minor A-shape barre chords at every position using the circle of fifths in the two exercises below.

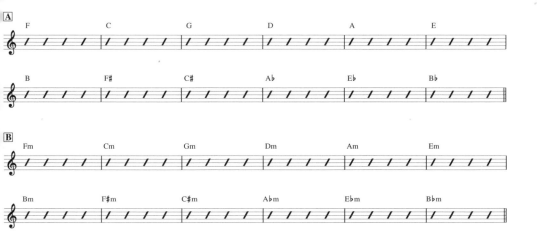

Now that you're familiar with playing these chords all over the fretboard, try your hand at these rock 'n' roll classics from Judas Priest, Eric Clapton, and the Guess Who.

LIVING AFTER MIDNIGHT

SHE'S WAITING

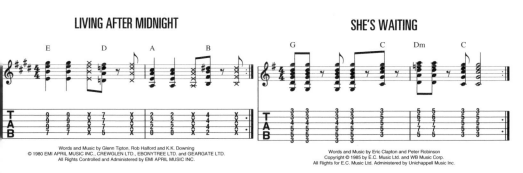

AMERICAN WOMAN

LEAD STUDY

As you may have guessed, there are major and minor scale fingerings that begin on the fifth string as well as the sixth string. Here are the two most popular fingerings used by rock guitar players.

Practice playing these scales—using strict alternate picking—all over the fretboard. Try following the circle of fifths as outlined in the chord practice example on page 41. Here are a few examples of how these scales are used in popular music.

WALK DON'T RUN

By Johnny Smith
Copyright © 1960 by Peermusic Ltd., On Board Music and Mesa Verde Music Co.
Copyright Renewed   All Rights Administered by Peermusic Ltd.

WHILE MY GUITAR GENTLY WEEPS

Words and Music by George Harrison
© 1968 HARRISONGS LTD.
Copyright Renewed 1997

BOHEMIAN RHAPSODY

Words and Music by Freddie Mercury
© 1975 B. FELDMAN & CO., LTD., Trading As TRIDENT MUSIC
All Rights Controlled and Administered by GLENWOOD MUSIC CORP.

HARMONICS

Fretted notes aren't the only notes on your guitar. By lightly touching a string over a specific fret while you pluck the string, you can produce a bell-like tone called a *harmonic*.

There are several "node" points along the length of the string that produce strong, resonant harmonics: the twelfth fret, the seventh fret, and the fifth fret. To produce a harmonic, lightly touch your finger to the string *directly* above one of these frets (rather than in between the frets). While your finger is touching the string, pluck the string with your pick and immediately lift your finger away from the string. The result should be a sustained ringing note. Try it on all six strings at the twelfth, seventh, and fifth frets.

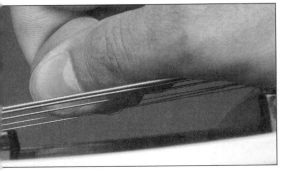

Yet another type of harmonic popular among rock guitarists is the *pinch* harmonic. To produce a pinch harmonic, you fret the note as usual, but you need to alter your pick hand attack. Choke down on your pick, so that only a small portion of the pick is exposed below your thumb and index finger. As you pick the string, allow your thumb to brush up against the string, creating a node point. The resulting sound should be a high-pitched harmonic. Using a lot of distortion will help bring out the harmonic, and varying the point of attack will produce different harmonics.

THE ATTITUDE SONG

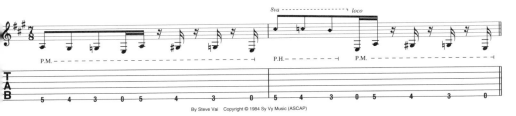

By Steve Vai   Copyright © 1984 Sy Vy Music (ASCAP)

DOWN BOYS

Words and Music by Jani Lane, Joey Allen, Jerry Dixon, Steven Sweet and Erik Turner
© 1989 EMI VIRGIN SONGS, INC., DICK DRAGON MUSIC, LIKITE SPLIT MUSIC, CRAB SALAD MUSIC, RICH MCBITCH MUSIC and GREAT LIPS MUSIC
All Rights Controlled and Administered by EMI VIRGIN SONGS, INC.

JAM SESSION

Long before the wave of female artists that reigned supreme in the '90s, there were the hard-rocking ladies the '80s—Joan Jett, the Wilson sisters of Heart, and above all, Pat Benatar. Her strong voice and equa strong video presence proved once and for all that women can indeed rock. If there's one song from her va catalog with which she'll always be synonymous, it's her 1980 smash "Hit Me with Your Best Shot."

Jam along with the rhythm track to practice your A-shape major and minor barre chords. Then solo to t track using either an E major scale or C# minor scale, utilizing the fingerings you learned in this chapter. T tossing a few trills and pinch harmonics into your solo for extra pizzazz.

HIT ME WITH YOUR BEST SHOT

CHAPTER 7: CLASSIC ROCK RHYTHMS

RHYTHM STUDY

Elvis Presley may be the "King," but Chuck Berry is the father of rock guitar. His rock 'n' roll rhythms chang the way guitar was played—and it endures to this day. Taking his cue from the blues guitar of Delta lege Robert Johnson, Berry propelled rock guitar into the spotlight with an energy and zest not unlike the fi piano antics of his contemporaries Little Richard and Jerry Lee Lewis.

In terms of rhythm guitar, Berry brought to the rock table the 5/6 chord pattern made popular by blues artis If you'll refer back to Chapter 3, in which you learned power chords, you should remember that a power ch is also called a fifth chord, or a "5" chord (e.g., E5), which is comprised of the root and perfect 5th from major scale. In open position, simply add your ring finger two frets above your index finger to play the ma 6th. The movable form is played with your index finger on the root note and your ring finger on the 5th. form the "6" chord, you stretch your pinky finger two frets above your ring finger and play the major 6th.

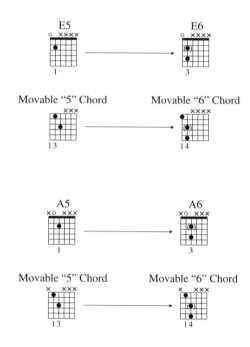

E5   E6

Movable "5" Chord   Movable "6" Chord

A5   A6

Movable "5" Chord   Movable "6" Chord

Progressions utilizing these types of chords were often played with a driving, straight-eighth feel. Try the Chuck Berry-style example below, and then give the next two classics a shot.

Chuck Berry-Style Rhythm

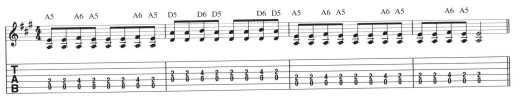

COME TOGETHER

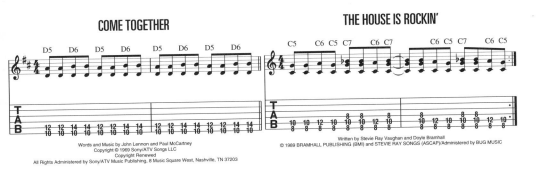

Words and Music by John Lennon and Paul McCartney
Copyright © 1969 Sony/ATV Songs LLC
Copyright Renewed
All Rights Administered by Sony/ATV Music Publishing, 8 Music Square West, Nashville, TN 37203

THE HOUSE IS ROCKIN'

Written by Stevie Ray Vaughan and Doyle Bramhall
© 1989 BRAMHALL PUBLISHING (BMI) and STEVIE RAY SONGS (ASCAP)/Administered by BUG MUSIC

Another mainstay in the classic rock rhythm is the *boogie bass* pattern—especially popular in early rock 'n' roll. Similar to bass lines, boogie bass patterns are typically played in open position, and they outline the chord changes using arpeggios. Here's the basic pattern from one of rock 'n' roll's best boogie moments.

JAILHOUSE ROCK

Words and Music by Jerry Leiber and Mike Stoller
© 1957 (Renewed) JERRY LEIBER MUSIC and MIKE STOLLER MUSIC

LEAD STUDY

Chuck Berry was also responsible for overhauling the way lead guitar was played. Champion of the *double* and *triple stop*—two or three notes played simultaneously—Berry would goose-step and duck-walk all over the fretboard. Double and triple stops are actually chords; only they're used in a lead guitar context. For double stops, intervals of 3rds and 4ths are most common. For triple stops, major and minor triads are the preferred choice. Here are the most popular shapes for double and triple stops:

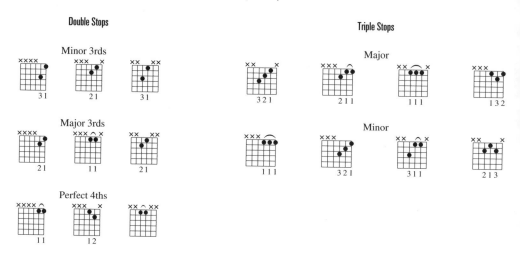

One of Berry's favorite techniques when playing double or triple stops was to play them with a triplet rhythm, sliding up to the notes on the downbeat. Try the following examples, starting only one or two frets away from the target notes and sliding very quickly into the double or triple stop.

Now, here are a few classic examples of double stops.

NO PARTICULAR PLACE TO GO

Words and Music by Chuck Berry   Copyright © 1964 (Renewed) by Arc Music Corporation (BMI)

PRIDE AND JOY

Written by Stevie Ray Vaughan   © 1985 RAY VAUGHAN MUSIC (ASCAP)/Administered by BUG MUSIC

JUMP, JIVE, AN' WAIL

Words and Music by Louis Prima   Copyright © 1956; Renewed and Assigned to LGL Music Co.   Administered by Larry Spier, Inc., New York

ADD STOPS TO YOUR RIFFS

Double and triple stops aren't just for lead guitar. You can use them in riffs or intertwine them into normal chord parts as well. You can also gain extra mileage out of them by using hammer-on and pull-off embellishments. Jimi Hendrix was a master of this. Try the Hendrix-like example below to get you started.

*Fret with thumb

JAM SESSION

An absolute cover-band classic, Bachman-Turner Overdrive's "Takin' Care of Business" gives Berry's traditional boogie pattern a makeover with strong accents and palm mutes creating a punchy rock rhythm. The song is in the key of F, but because the progression begins on the V chord (C5), it also has a key-of-C feel. As such, when you're ready to try soloing over the progression, try using both the C minor and C major pentatonic scales in your solo. In the first chorus, play from C minor, and in the second chorus, play from C major. Also, be sure to throw in plenty of double stops, triple stops, and embellishments.

TRACK 8

TAKIN' CARE OF BUSINESS

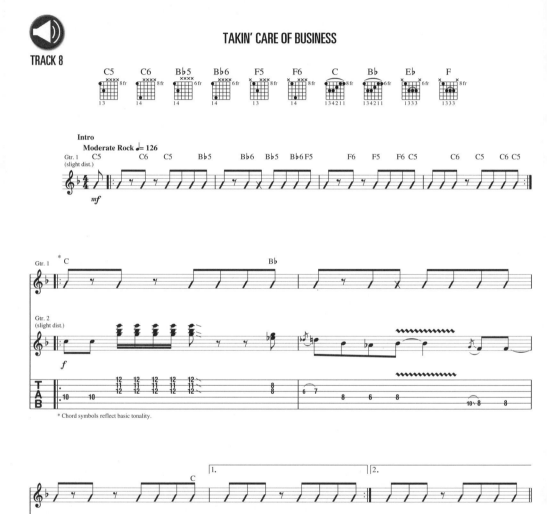

* Chord symbols reflect basic tonality.

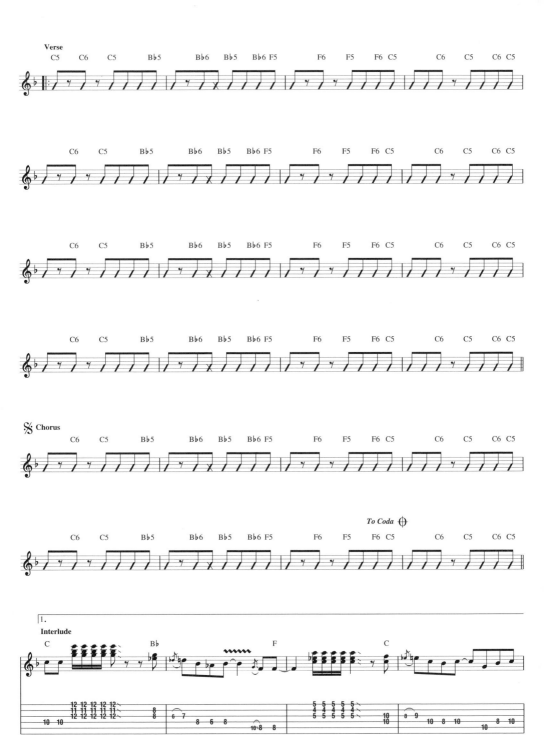

CHAPTER 8: BLUES/ROCK

RHYTHM STUDY

Rock 'n' roll, and thus rock guitar, was largely born out of blues music. As such, it's appropriate to talk a little about blues guitar and its influence on the rock style. In terms of rhythm guitar, the blues brought forth the *dominant seventh* chord. The dominant seventh chord is built by adding the flatted seventh scale tone to a major triad. Thus, a C7 chord (C–E–G–Bb) is simply a C major chord (C–E–G) with the Bb note added. Here are a few of the most popular movable dominant seventh chord fingerings:

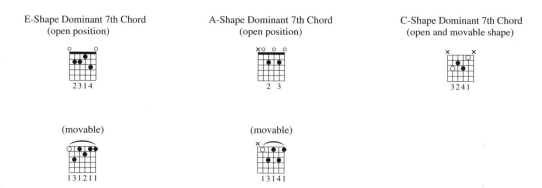

E-Shape Dominant 7th Chord (open position)

2 3 1 4

A-Shape Dominant 7th Chord (open position)

2   3

C-Shape Dominant 7th Chord (open and movable shape)

3 2 4 1

(movable)

1 3 1 2 1 1

(movable)

1 3 1 4 1

Notice that the first chord shape is based on the E-shape barre chord you learned in Chapter 4. The second one is based on the A-shape barre chord you learned in Chapter 6. Finally, the third shape is the same as the open C chord from Chapter 1, but here, you add your pinky finger to the third string. Here's a 12-bar blues in the key of A using each of these chord shapes.

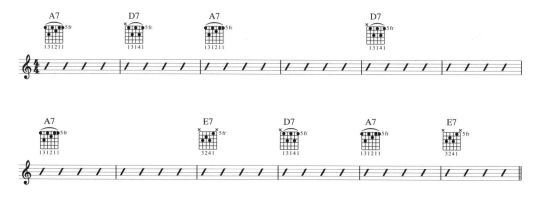

Of course, you could play that 12-bar blues using any one of those three shapes and simply move it up and down the fretboard. Try playing the previous song three times, using only one chord shape (E-shape, A-shape, C-shape) each time. Then, work your way through a chorus of the legendary B.B. King's "Everyday (I Have the Blues)."

EVERYDAY (I HAVE THE BLUES)

In addition to the dominant seventh chord, the blues also introduced rock 'n' roll to the *shuffle* feel. A shuffle is notated in eighth notes, yet has the feel of playing eighth-note triplets with the first two eighth notes tied together.

The Shuffle Feel

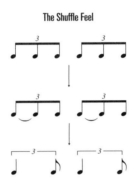

Do you remember that in Chapter 7, Classic Rock Rhythms, we discussed the 5/6 chord pattern made popular in rock music by Chuck Berry? Well, it was first made popular by Delta blues artists such as Robert Johnson in the 1930s. In fact, Johnson's "Sweet Home Chicago" is one of the most noted recordings using this now-famous chord pattern—only Johnson's version used the shuffle feel. In fact, Johnson used not only 5th and 6th chords in his pattern, he also used seventh chords, which are formed by moving the higher note of the 6th chord up one fret.

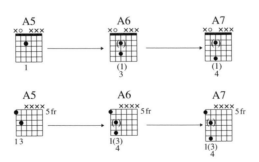

Here are two riffs that use the shuffle feel. The first is the timeless blues "Sweet Home Chicago," and the second is a great example of how rock guitar has adopted these sounds for itself, as heard in the Allman Brothers' "Statesboro Blues."

SWEET HOME CHICAGO

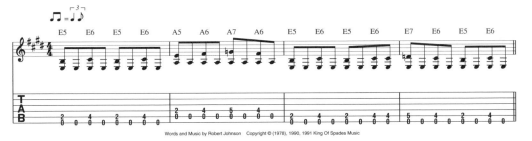

Words and Music by Robert Johnson   Copyright © (1978), 1990, 1991 King Of Spades Music

STATESBORO BLUES

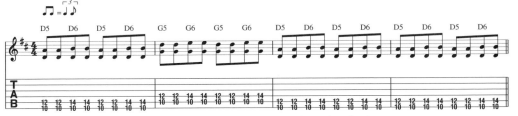

Words and Music by Willy McTell   Copyright © 1929 by Peer International Corporation   Copyright Renewed

LEAD STUDY

If you're going to incorporate blues-based music into your rock guitar stylings, it's imperative that you become very familiar with the blues scale. Containing six notes, the blues scale is very similar to the minor pentatonic scale except that it adds the flatted fifth degree of the scale, which is sometimes referred to as the "blue note." Here is the most common box fingering of the blues scale.

Blues scale (movable box)

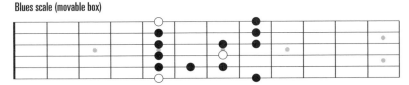

There are countless examples in the blues where the blues scale is used to build a riff or a signature lick. Here are a couple of the more famous ones from blues guitar luminary Stevie Ray Vaughan.

SCUTTLE BUTTIN'

Written by Stevie Ray Vaughan
© 1984 RAY VAUGHAN MUSIC (ASCAP)/Administered by BUG MUSIC

55

COULDN'T STAND THE WEATHER

Obviously, you can use the blues scale when you're playing a blues song, but you can also get a lot of mileage out of it in a rock context as well, whether it be in a riff or in a solo. Following are some of rock guitar's greatest riffs, all relying on the blues scale to convey their rock 'n' roll messages.

WALK THIS WAY

SUNSHINE OF YOUR LOVE

ROCK AND ROLL HOOCHIE KOO

REPEATING LICKS

A common rock guitar soloing tool, also borrowed from the blues, is the repeating lick. Repeating licks are excellent tools for building excitement into your solos. They can be heard in such memorable solos as "Rock and Roll" by Led Zeppelin and "Freebird" by Lynyrd Skynyrd. To create your own, find a lick that fits within the context of one or two beats (without rests), and cycle it four to eight times. The important thing is that it fits within the rhythm. Here are a couple of old blues-rock reliables to get you started.

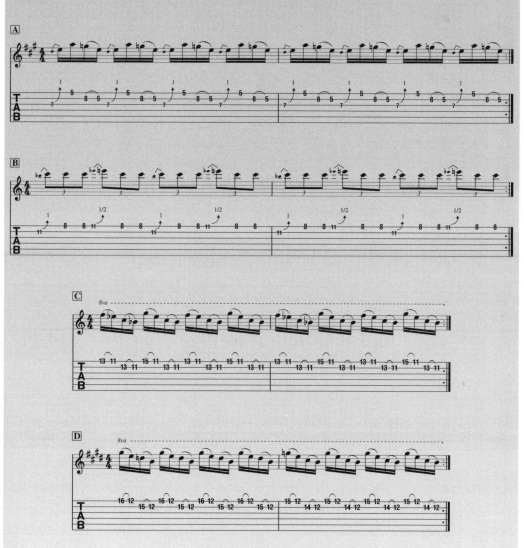

JAM SESSION

Stevie Ray Vaughan is one of only a handful of artists, joining the likes of Jimi Hendrix and Eric Clapton, to find critical success in both the blues and rock guitar arenas. His rock-edged Texas blues sound and style set the standard for virtuoso blues-rock guitar.

One of his signature songs, "Pride and Joy," combines the use of an open-position riff with strummed chords on the upbeats. In this arrangement, use the seventh chord fingerings you learned in this chapter to jam along with the rhythm part. Then, use the E blues scale in both open and twelfth position to solo over the chord changes.

PRIDE AND JOY

TRACK 9

Written by Stevie Ray Vaughan
© 1985 RAY VAUGHAN MUSIC (ASCAP)/Administered by BUG MUSIC

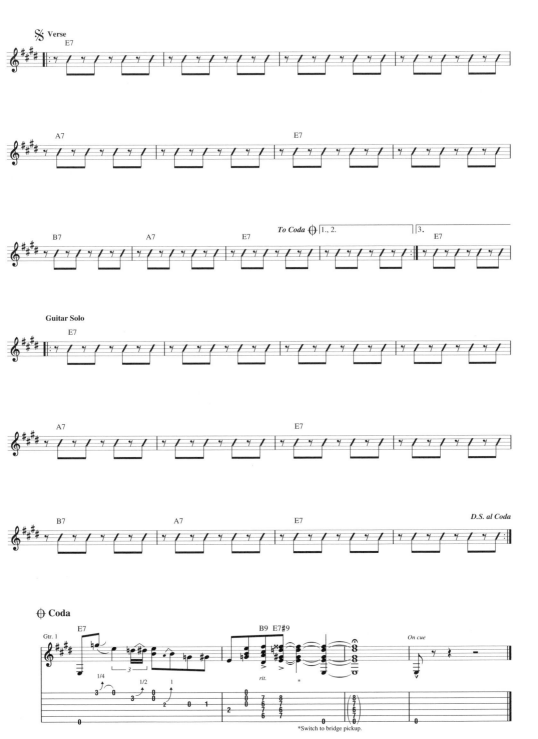

CHAPTER 9: ROCK BALLADS

RHYTHM STUDY

The rock ballad has been a pervasive song style ever since rock 'n' roll's inception in the 1950s. The rock ballad is often characterized by the use of arpeggios in the chord progression and moderately slow tempos, often combined with a 6/8 or 12/8 meter.

An *arpeggio* is a chord that is played one note at a time. For example, place your fret-hand fingers in position to play an open C major chord. Now, instead of strumming the chord in one action, play it as written in the example below.

As you can see in the example above, the chord tones don't have to be played in intervallic order when you play arpeggios. This is a very common variation on arpeggios in popular music. For more practice playing arpeggios, try playing all of the open chords and barre chords that you've learned in arpeggio format. Once you've become comfortable with picking single strings within the chord shapes, try the following rock riffs.

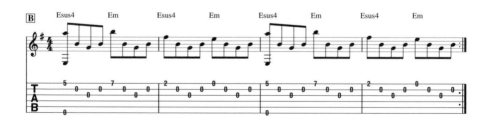

Eric Clapton's "Wonderful Tonight" practically defines a rock ballad. Through the years, it has become one of the most popular ballads of all time.

WONDERFUL TONIGHT

In the 1980s, a new type of rock ballad, coined the "power ballad," emerged from the hearts of heavy metal bands like Poison, Motley Crue, and Cinderella. Here is Cinderella's "Nobody's Fool," a prime example of the new classic power ballad.

NOBODY'S FOOL

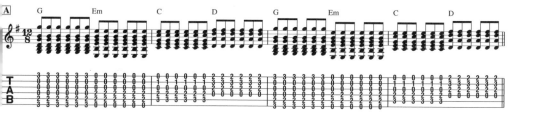

Those two riffs contained two classic elements of a rock ballad: slow tempo and arpeggios. Now, let's take a look at the third element: the 12/8 or 6/8 time signature. Earlier, you learned that a 4/4 time signature contains four quarter-note beats in a measure. The 12/8 meter contains twelve eighth-notes, where the eighth note gets the pulse, and the 6/8 meter contains six eighth-notes. The next two examples utilize the I–vi–IV–V chord progression—a rock ballad staple—in the style of 1950s ballads such as "Earth Angel." In the first, strum the chords on every beat, just to get used to the eighth-note pulse. In the second, play the chords in arpeggio format.

LEAD STUDY

You can also use arpeggios in a soloing context. After all, chords are constructed from scales, and we use scales for solos, so why not use arpeggios in your solos? Using arpeggios in a solo not only helps to keep you "in touch" with the song's chord progression, it also serves as a wonderful reference point for the listener.

One of the easiest ways to incorporate arpeggios into your solos is to use triad versions of the chords from the rhythm part. Take a look at the progression below. It's a very common rock progression over which you could use notes from the F major scale for your solo. If you study the short solo that accompanies the progression, you'll see that, indeed, all the notes are from the F major scale, but there are several arpeggios worked in as well to help outline the chord changes.

Arpeggios have played an integral role in riffs and solos of many of rock's greatest songs. Here, they play a major role in these timeless pieces from Dire Straits, the Allman Brothers, and Stevie Ray Vaughan.

SULTANS OF SWING

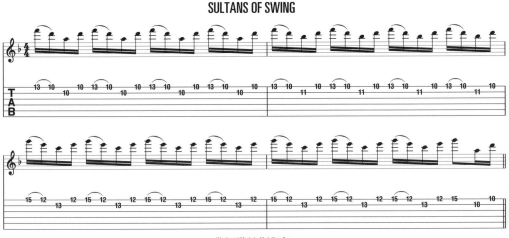

Words and Music by Mark Knopfler
Copyright © 1978 Straitjacket Songs Ltd.

JESSICA

Written by Dickey Betts
Copyright © 1973 by Unichappell Music Inc. and F.R. Betts Music Co.
All Rights Administered by Unichappell Music Inc.

RIVIERA PARADISE

Written by Stevie Ray Vaughan
© 1984 RAY VAUGHAN MUSIC (ASCAP)/Administered by BUG MUSIC

VOLUME SWELLS

A wonderful technique to embellish and enhance melody lines in a ballad is the *volume swell*. This effect can be achieved in one of two ways: a volume pedal or your guitar's volume control knob. In either case, the concept is the same. With your volume off, strike a note and then gradually turn up the volume. Playing in this manner masks the pick attack, thus giving the note an almost violin-like timbre.

A good way to practice volume swells is by playing scales exclusively with volume swells. Below is the F major scale. Practice the technique and then try to incorporate volume swells into your solo over "Time Is on My Side" in this chapter's Jam Session

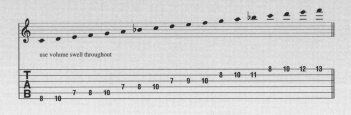

use volume swell throughout

JAM SESSION

The Rolling Stones are considered by many as one of the greatest rock bands to ever take the stage. Their vast catalog contains everything from all-out rockers to blues and country flavors to, of course, the rock ballad. "Time Is on My Side" is an ageless rock ballad in 6/8 time. As an added bonus, this song will provide you extra practice using barre chords. Once you're comfortable with the 6/8 feel and strumming along with the chords, try playing the chords in arpeggiated fashion. Then, try soloing over the form using the F major and F major pentatonic scales. Be sure to work in some arpeggios during your solo.

TRACK 10

TIME IS ON MY SIDE

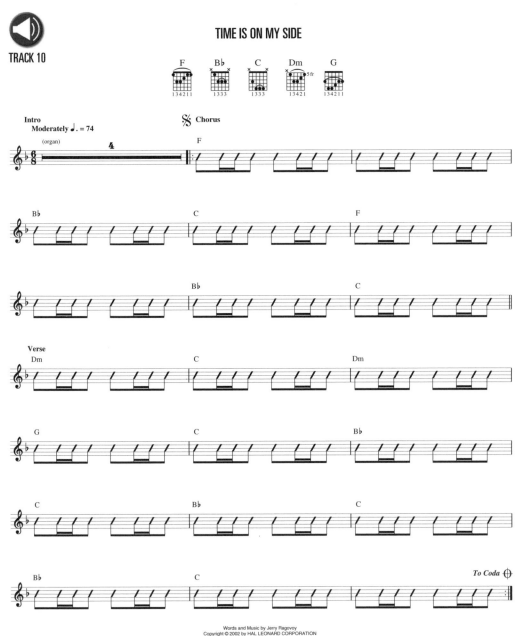

Words and Music by Jerry Ragovoy
Copyright © 2002 by HAL LEONARD CORPORATION

CLOSING

That wraps up the Hal Leonard Rock Guitar method. Let's take a moment to review all that you've accomplished. In learning the basic theory and techniques necessary to play rock guitar, you've also learned to play songs from rock's biggest artists, including the Beatles, Eric Clapton, Black Sabbath, Carlos Santana, and many, many more. Perhaps more importantly, you've discovered that rock guitar does not have to be complex, and that a simple idea and simple technique can yield moving, timeless music to be enjoyed for generations of rock guitar players to come. In other words, you can do it!

I hope you've enjoyed working through this method. As a committed rock guitarist, you should realize that learning and practicing never end. Although you've reached the end of this book, you're not finished using it yet. You can always revisit these lessons to better understand the concepts and better use the techniques presented herein until you're confident that you've mastered them. Good luck with your musical progress, and be sure to check out the Hal Leonard catalog for new materials to further your study of rock guitar.

Guitar Notation Legend

Guitar Music can be notated three different ways: on a *musical staff*, in *tablature*, and in *rhythm slashes*.

RHYTHM SLASHES are written above the staff. Strum chords in the rhythm indicated. Use the chord diagrams found at the top of the first page of the transcription for the appropriate chord voicings. Round noteheads indicate single notes.

THE MUSICAL STAFF shows pitches and rhythms and is divided by bar lines into measures. Pitches are named after the first seven letters of the alphabet.

TABLATURE graphically represents the guitar fingerboard. Each horizontal line represents a a string, and each number represents a fret.

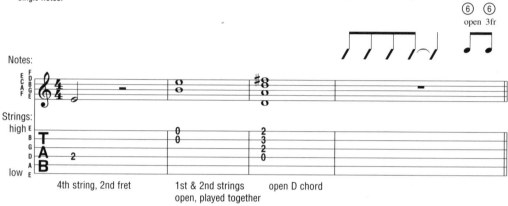

4th string, 2nd fret

1st & 2nd strings open, played together

open D chord

Definitions for Special Guitar Notation

HALF-STEP BEND: Strike the note and bend up 1/2 step.

WHOLE-STEP BEND: Strike the note and bend up one step.

GRACE NOTE BEND: Strike the note and immediately bend up as indicated.

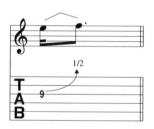

SLIGHT (MICROTONE) BEND: Strike the note and bend up 1/4 step.

BEND AND RELEASE: Strike the note and bend up as indicated, then release back to the original note. Only the first note is struck.

PRE-BEND: Bend the note as indicated, then strike it.

PRE-BEND AND RELEASE: Bend the note as indicated. Strike it and release the bend back to the original note.

UNISON BEND: Strike the two notes simultaneously and bend the lower note up to the pitch of the higher.

VIBRATO: The string is vibrated by rapidly bending and releasing the note with the fretting hand.

WIDE VIBRATO: The pitch is varied to a greater degree by vibrating with the fretting hand.

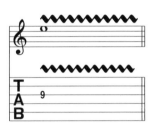

HAMMER-ON: Strike the first (lower) note with one finger, then sound the higher note (on the same string) with another finger by fretting it without picking.

PULL-OFF: Place both fingers on the notes to be sounded. Strike the first note and without picking, pull the finger off to sound the second (lower) note.

LEGATO SLIDE: Strike the first note and then slide the same fret-hand finger up or down to the second note. The second note is not struck.

SHIFT SLIDE: Same as legato slide, except the second note is struck.

TRILL: Very rapidly alternate between the notes indicated by continuously hammering on and pulling off.

TAPPING: Hammer ("tap") the fret indicated with the pick-hand index or middle finger and pull off to the note fretted by the fret hand.

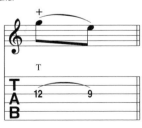

NATURAL HARMONIC: Strike the note while the fret-hand lightly touches the string directly over the fret indicated.

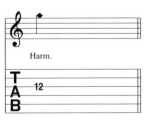

PINCH HARMONIC: The note is fretted normally and a harmonic is produced by adding the edge of the thumb or the tip of the index finger of the pick hand to the normal pick attack.

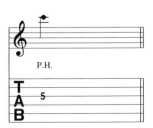

HARP HARMONIC: The note is fretted normally and a harmonic is produced by gently resting the pick hand's index finger directly above the indicated fret (in parentheses) while the pick hand's thumb or pick assists by plucking the appropriate string.

PICK SCRAPE: The edge of the pick is rubbed down (or up) the string, producing a scratchy sound.

MUFFLED STRINGS: A percussive sound is produced by laying the fret hand across the string(s) without depressing, and striking them with the pick hand.

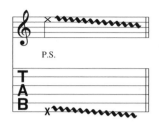

PALM MUTING: The note is partially muted by the pick hand lightly touching the string(s) just before the bridge.

RAKE: Drag the pick across the strings indicated with a single motion.

TREMOLO PICKING: The note is picked as rapidly and continuously as possible.

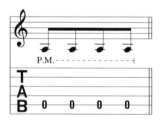

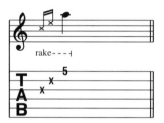

ARPEGGIATE: Play the notes of the chord indicated by quickly rolling them from bottom to top.

VIBRATO BAR DIVE AND RETURN: The pitch of the note or chord is dropped a specified number of steps (in rhythm) then returned to the original pitch.

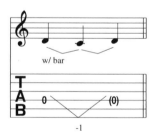

VIBRATO BAR SCOOP: Depress the bar just before striking the note, then quickly release the bar.

VIBRATO BAR DIP: Strike the note and then immediately drop a specified number of steps, then release back to the original pitch.

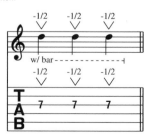

Additional Musical Definitions

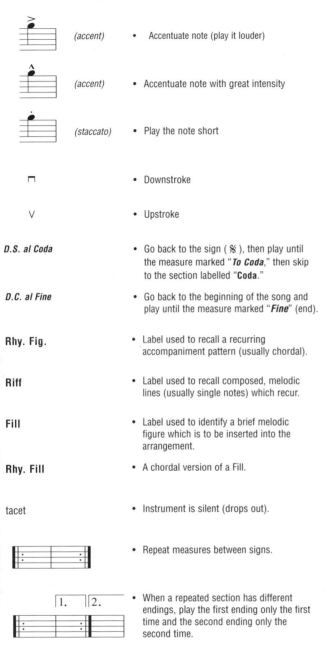

(accent)	•	Accentuate note (play it louder)
(accent)	•	Accentuate note with great intensity
(staccato)	•	Play the note short
	•	Downstroke
	•	Upstroke

D.S. al Coda • Go back to the sign (𝄋), then play until the measure marked "*To Coda*," then skip to the section labelled "**Coda**."

D.C. al Fine • Go back to the beginning of the song and play until the measure marked "***Fine***" (end).

Rhy. Fig. • Label used to recall a recurring accompaniment pattern (usually chordal).

Riff • Label used to recall composed, melodic lines (usually single notes) which recur.

Fill • Label used to identify a brief melodic figure which is to be inserted into the arrangement.

Rhy. Fill • A chordal version of a Fill.

tacet • Instrument is silent (drops out).

• Repeat measures between signs.

• When a repeated section has different endings, play the first ending only the first time and the second ending only the second time.

NOTE: Tablature numbers in parentheses mean:
1. The note is being sustained over a system (note in standard notation is tied), or
2. The note is sustained, but a new articulation (such as a hammer-on, pull-off, slide or vibrato begins), or
3. The note is a barely audible "ghost" note (note in standard notation is also in parentheses).

HAL LEONARD GUITAR METHOD

MORE THAN A METHOD...
IT'S A SYSTEM!

This comprehensive method is preferred by teachers and students alike for many reasons: • Learning sequence is carefully paced with clear instructions that make it easy to learn. • Popular songs increase the incentive to learn to play. • Versatile enough to be used as self-instruction or with a teacher. • Audio accompaniments let students have fun and sound great while practicing.

METHOD BOOKS

BOOK 1
Book 1 provides beginning instruction which covers: tuning; playing position; musical symbols; notes in first position; the C, G, G7, D, D7, A7 and Em chords; rhythms through eighth notes; strumming and picking; 100 great songs; riffs and examples. Added features are a chord chart and a selection of well-known songs, including "Ode to Joy," "Rockin' Robin," "Greensleeves," "Give My Regards to Broadway," and "Time Is on My Side."
00699010 Book $5.95
00699027 Book/CD Pack $9.95

BOOK 2
Book 2 continues the instruction started in Book 1 and covers: Am, Dm, A, E, F and B7 chords; power chords; finger-style guitar; syncopations, dotted rhythms, and triplets; Carter-style solos; bass runs; pentatonic scales; improvising; tablature; 92 great songs, riffs and examples; notes in first and second position; and more! The CD includes 57 full-band tracks for demonstration or play-along.
00699020 Book $5.95
00697313 Book/CD Pack $9.95

BOOK 3
Book 3 covers: the major, minor, pentatonic and chromatic scales; sixteenth notes; barre chords; drop D tuning; movable scales; notes in fifth position; slides, hammer-ons, pull-offs and string bends; chord construction; gear; 90 great songs, riffs and examples; and more! The CD includes 61 full-band tracks for demonstration or play-along.
00699030 Book $5.95
00697316 Book/CD Pack $9.95

COMPOSITE
Books 1, 2, and 3 bound together in an easy-to-use spiral binding.
00699040 Book $14.95
00697342 Book/CD $22.95

HAL LEONARD GUITAR METHOD VIDEO AND DVD
For the beginning electric or acoustic guitarist
00697318 DVD $19.9

SONGBOOKS

EASY POP RHYTHMS
Strum along with your favorite hits from the Beatles, the Rolling Stones, the Eagles and more!
00697336 Book $5.95
00697309 Book/CD Pack $14.95

MORE EASY POP RHYTHMS
00697338 Book $5.95
00697322 Book/CD Pack $14.95

EVEN MORE EASY POP RHYTHMS
00697340 Book $5.95
00697323 Book/CD Pack $14.95

EASY POP MELODIES
Play along with your favorite hits from the Beatles, Elton John, Elvis Presley, the Police, Nirvana and more!
00697281 Book $5.95
00697268 Book/CD Pack $14.95

MORE EASY POP MELODIES
00697280 Book $5.95
00697269 Book/CD Pack $14.95

EVEN MORE EASY POP MELODIES
00699154 Book $5.95
00697270 Book/CD Pack $14.9

STYLISTIC METHODS

BLUES GUITAR
by Greg Koch
This book teaches the basics of blues guitar in the style of B.B. King, Stevie Ray Vaughan, Buddy Guy, Muddy Waters and more.
00697326 Book/CD Pack $12.95

COUNTRY GUITAR
by Greg Koch
This book teaches the basics of country guitar in the styles of Chet Atkins, Albert Lee, Merle Travis and more.
00697337 Book/CD Pack $12.95

JAZZ GUITAR
by Jeff Schroedl
This book teaches the basics of jazz guitar in the style of Wes Montgomery, Joe Pass, Tal Farlow, Charlie Christian, Jim Hall and more.
00695359 Book/CD Pack $12.95

ROCK GUITAR
by Michael Mueller
This book teaches the basics of rock guitar in the style of Eric Clapton, the Beatles, the Rolling Stones and many others.
00697319 Book/CD Pack $12.95

Visit Hal Leonard Online at
www.halleonard.com

HAL•LEONARD®
CORPORATION
7777 W. BLUEMOUND RD. P.O. BOX 13819 MILWAUKEE, WI 53213

Prices, contents and availability subject to change without notice.